REFORMS: TAX, ADMINISTRATIVE AND POLITICAL

REFORMS

TAX, ADMINISTRATIVE AND POLITICAL

Current tax, administrative and
political system

Osvaldo Dalla Coletta

Santo André, 2023

Layout | Israel Dias de Oliveira
Translation | Icaro Bagolan
Revision | Débora Beltrão

International Cataloging-in-Publication (CIP) Data
(Câmara Brasileira do Livro, SP, Brazil)
Aline Graziele Benitez - Librarian - CRB-1/3129

Coletta, Osvaldo Dalla
  Tax, administrative and political reforms : current tax, administrative and political system / Osvaldo Dalla Coletta. – 1st ed. – Santo André, São Paulo, Brazil: Published by the Author, 2023.

  ISBN 978-65-00-66113-2

  1. Public administration 2. Tax law 3. Public finances 4. Taxes - Brazil - Legislation 5. Tax reform 6. National Tax System (Brazil) I. Title.

23-150374   CDU-34:336.2(81)

Index for systematic cataloging:
1. Brazil : Tax reform : Tax law 34:336.2(81)

[2023]

SUMMARY

TAX REFORM

DEFINITIONS

Levies: in the current Brazilian tax system, levies consist of taxes, fees and contributions. At present (February 2023), there are ninety-two (92) different taxes in Brazil.

IU: Single Tax (IU, for the acronym in Portuguese of Imposto Único).

Single Tax (IU): Tax to be instituted by this tax reform to replace all 92 taxes currently existing in Brazil. The one exception is the import tax, which is expected to survive given that it is a regulatory, antidumping measure. The total amount of IU to be charged is the sum of the federal, district, state and municipal budgets for the current month.

National Revenue Service: Administrative agency resulting from the transformation of the Federal Revenue Service into the National Revenue Service to collect the IU, i.e. the tax amounts provided for in the federal, district, state and municipal budgets, to be collected from individuals residing in Brazil. Every year, the federal, district, state and municipal governments send the budgets approved by their legislatures to the National Revenue Service.

Algorithm: Logical sequence of instructions, written in computer programming language, to produce a certain result. For example, to calculate 2 x 3 = 6, the computer programmer writes a logical sequence of instructions in programming language, equivalent to what you do with a manual calculator when you press the keys (2), (x), (3) and (=), to get 6.

Tax Domicile: An individual's address on file with the National Revenue Service. The National Revenue Service's electronic processing system algorithm uses the postal code of that taxpayer to identify the state or Federal District and the municipality in which the taxpayer resides, to credit the state's or Federal District's IU to the state's or Federal District's bank account, and to credit the municipality's IU to the municipality's bank account. Municipal governments are responsible for updating individual's addresses in the National Revenue Service's records.

Tax Statement: Individual monthly digital statement generated by the National Revenue Service and sent to the email address of each individual on file with the National Revenue Service. This tax statement contains the date of the statement, the individuals' name and Individual Taxpayer Number (CPF) the amount of IU paid to each of the federal, state or district and municipal governments, and total IU paid.

Taxpayers: Only individuals are taxpayers, as they are the end consumers who buy and pay the prices of products and services, prices that include taxes. Legal entities (companies) are not end consumers, therefore they do not pay taxes, because under the Brazilian current tax system they only collect the taxes embedded in the sales price of the products and services that are bought and paid by individuals, who are the end consumers, as shown in the following example.

Example with taxes from the Brazilian current tax system:

Product cost = R$100.00
+ 10% profit = R$111.11 (100.00/0.90 = 111.11)
Product price = R$111.11 (before taxes)
+ 13% IPI = R$16.60 (111.11/0.87 = 127.71 – 111.11 = 16.60)
+ 18% ICMS = R$24.39 (111.11/0.82 = 135.50 – 111.11 = 24.39)
Product price = R$152.07 (for the end consumer)

When an end consumer buys the product in the above example, they pay the total amount of R$152.07 to the legal entity (company), where R$111.11 is the product price, R$16.60 is for Excise Tax (IPI) and R$24.39 is the State Goods and Services Tax (ICMS). The legal entity (company) collects R$16.60 in IPI to remit to the federal government, R$24.39 of ICMS to remit to the state or district government, and keeps R$111.11.

Tax base: Financial amount over which the tax rate (%) is applied to obtain the amount of tax to be collected from taxpayers.

Tax progressivity: Tax progressivity is a proportional tax system where each taxpayer pays according to their ability to pay. In other words, it is proportional to taxpayer income, charging more from those who earn more and less from those who earn less.

Dumping: Unfair commercial practice that occurs when a certain imported product arrives in the importing country for a price that is lower than the cost of the product in the exporting country. In this case, import tax is levied so that the cost of this imported product is equal to its cost in the exporting country.

CPF: Individual Taxpayer Registration in Brazil (CPF, for the acronym in Portuguese of Cadastro de Pessoa Física).

Sole Proprietor Microenterprise (MEI): Any individual (CPF) currently operating as an investor to buy and sell movable and immovable goods, such as cars, real estate, and company shares, will need to operate as a legal entity (MEI) after this tax reform is approved by the National Congress.

Payments made to individuals: In the verbiage of this tax reform, "payments" includes transfers for any purpose, such as loans and donations.

Federal District: Under this tax reform, the federal district will be considered a state.

TAX REFORM

Tax reform to replace all 92 Brazilian taxes with a Single Tax (IU), to be levied on all individuals residing in Brazil. The one exception is the import tax, which must be maintained as a regulatory, antidumping measure.

The IU tax base for each individual is the total gross monthly income of the individual less the equivalent to one minimum monthly wage. IU will be collected automatically by the National Revenue Service's electronic processing system, by withholding it at the source when payments are made to individuals. By the fifth working day of each month, the algorithm of the National Revenue Service's electronic processing system will add up all the amounts withheld from an individual in the previous month, and subtract from that sum the value corresponding to one minimum monthly wage, thus arriving at the calculation basis of IU — and, considering this tax base, will select the applicable rate from a progressive gross income range table corresponding to the tax base amount obtained to calculate the IU payable in the prior month. When there is a difference between the total monthly amount withheld in the prior month and the total monthly amount payable in such month, the difference will be debited or credited to the individual's CPF. When the tax base is equal or lower than one minimum monthly wage in the prior month, no IU is due, and the total amount withheld in the prior month is credited to the individual's CPF.

The total amount of IU to be collected from taxpayers are the amounts listed in the federal, state and municipal government budgets for the current month. First the algorithm collects the tax to match the amount listed in the federal government's budget for the current month. Then the algorithm uses the postal code on file with the Internal Revenue Service to identify the municipality and the state where the individual resides and collects the amounts listed in the state and municipal budgets for the current month.

The tax amounts listed in federal, state, and local budgets to be collected by the National Revenue Service through the Single Tax (IU) will be credited automatically and directly to the bank accounts of the federal, state and municipal governments when withheld at the source.

The Single Tax (IU) will be charged based on the progressive table below:

Minimum Monthly Wages	Rates (%)
0-1	1
1-2	2
2-3	3
3-4	4
4-5	5
5-6	6
6-7	7
7-8	8
8-9	9
9-10	10
10-11	11
11-12	12
12-13	13
13-14	14
14-15	15
15-16	16
16-17	17
17-18	18
18-19	19
19-20	20
20-21	21

21-22	22
22-23	23
23-24	24
24-25	25
25-26	26
26-27	27
27-28	28
Over 28	29

The algorithm of the National Revenue Service's electronic processing system will control collection on a daily basis to collect the amount listed in the federal, state and municipal government budgets, —no more, no less — and, if necessary, will make daily adjustments to the progressive rates, increasing or decreasing them so that the amount collected equals the amounts in the federal, state and municipal government budgets, regardless of upward or downward changes in economic activity. To make daily adjustments to the progressive table rates, the algorithm uses statistical data from the collection of each day of the month in the quarter prior to the current month and the amount to be collected for each day of the current month.

The electronic records of the payments made to individuals will be created in real time (online), directly on the National Revenue Service's website. These electronic records contain the total payment amount, the amount IU withheld for the federal, state and municipal governments, the payer's CNPJ or CPF, the payee's CPF, and a code with other information required by the National Revenue Service and the Brazilian Institute of Geography and Statistics (IBGE). When payments to individuals cannot be recorded in real time (online), payers will make electronic records of these payments at the end of each day or at the end of each week.

After Congressional approval and implementation, this tax reform guarantees that the federal, state and municipal governments will have their revenues preserved.

After this tax reform is approved and implemented, the federal, state and municipal governments will be prohibited from: granting tax immunity and exemptions, collecting more than is allocated in their budgets, spending more than taxes collected, borrowing money, lending money and being a borrower's guarantor. These same governments will also be required to pay off all their existing debts within twenty (20) years, at a minimum of 1/20 per year, as well as to collect all their tax credits within twenty years.

When taxpayers want to lower their tax burden, they should contact their legislative representatives and have them pass budgets for the following year that reduce such burden.

Considering that the federal, state and municipal governments will not be able to collect more than allocated in the budget, nor spend more than they collect, they will be required to create a financial reserve fund, earmarked to cover expenses arising from natural disasters and health emergencies as well as to take out a subsidiary liability insurance policy for each government project they execute, to ensure the good quality of the public tender notice and project design, structural soundness, timely delivery, as well as to ensure the payment of any third-party claims until the end of the warranty period of each government project contracted.

The insurance company will work to prevent: flaws in the public tender notice, design flaws, construction defects, late delivery of each insured government project and any third-party damages. While the construction company's lead engineer for each government project contracted by the federal, state and municipal governments will remain responsible for the project, the insurer will have its own secondary lead engineer for each insured government project, as a preventive measure to avoid any fines late delivery and to assume the financial losses resulting from flaws in the public tender notice, project design flaws, structural defects, repairs and any third-party claims until the end of the warranty period of each insured government project.

While the construction company's lead engineer will continue to oversee the work, the insurance company's secondary lead engineer for the insured government project will have the following rights: participate in drafting the public tender, participate in drafting the project and having free access to the construction site of the insured government project until construction is completed and the government project delivered. The participation of the insurer's secondary lead engineer during the drafting phase of the public tender notice is important to prevent possible technical failures such as, for example, to ensure the correct technical specifications of the macadam when paving roads, avenues and streets, in other words (the weight of each vehicle plus its maximum load), to prevent the surface from warping and cracking shortly after pavement is laid.

After this tax reform is approved and implemented by Congress, legal entities (companies) will only make the monthly deposit of each worker's Guarantee Fund for Length of Service (FGTS) and, when applicable, will collect import tax. Payroll, the sale and provision of services, and the manufacturing, sale and transport of machines, products and goods will be fully exempt from taxes and free of any bureaucratic constraints imposed by the government.

This tax reform, once approved and implemented, guarantees that the federal, state and municipal governments have their revenues preserved and also ensures the fiscal autonomy of states and municipalities by eliminating the current fiscal dependency caused by the transfers of federal revenues to states, and from states to municipalities.

When taxpayers want to lower their tax burden, they should contact their legislative representatives and have them pass budgets for the following year that reduce such burden.

CURRENT TAX SYSTEM

Under the current Brazilian tax system, only individuals are taxpayers, as they are the end consumers of products, goods and services. Legal entities (companies) are not taxpayers, therefore they do not pay taxes, they only collect the taxes included in the price of the products and services bought and paid by individuals, who are the end consumers of all products and services sold.

For example:

Product cost = R$100.00

+ 10% profit = R$111.11 (100.00/0.90 = 111.11)

Product price = R$111.11 (before taxes)

+ 13% IPI = R$16.60 (111.11/0.87 = 127.71 – 111.11 = 16.60)

+ 18% ICMS = R$24.39 (111.11/0.82 = 135.50 – 111.11 = 24.39)

Product price = R$152.10 (for the end consumer)

When an end consumer buys the product in the above example, they pay the total amount of R$152.07 to the legal entity (company), where R$111.11 is the product price, R$16.60 is for Excise Tax (IPI) and R$24.39 is the Value-Added Tax on Sales and Services (ICMS). The legal entity (company) collects R$16.60 in IPI to remit to the federal government, R$24.39 of ICMS to remit to the state or district government, and keeps R$111.11.

In the industrial sector, product cost is the sum of all variable costs and all fixed costs used to manufacture a given product.

Variable costs are determined by raw materials, whose quantities and costs vary according to the quantities produced. For example, the total cost of electric motors for blenders varies according to the quantity of blenders produced.

Fixed costs do not vary according to the quantities produced. For example, the Urban Property Tax (IPTU) for the blender factory's warehouse is always the same, regardless of how many blenders are produced. The distribution (apportionment) of fixed costs by product is equal to the manufacturing cost of the product multiplied by the fixed cost distribution (apportionment) factor. The distribution factor (apportionment) is obtained by dividing the sum of the production costs of products manufactured in the current month by the sum of the fixed costs for the current month.

In commerce, cost is equal to the purchase cost of the product to be sold plus fixed cost. The distribution (apportionment) of fixed cost by product is equal to the purchase cost of each product purchased multiplied by the fixed cost distribution (apportionment) factor. The distribution factor (apportionment) is obtained by dividing the sum of the values of products purchased in the current month by the sum of the fixed costs for the current month.

Brazil's current tax system (as of February 2023) has 92 levies that encompass taxes, fees and contributions.

Paying taxes is an obligation that must be fulfilled by taxpayers when the taxable event occurs. One example of a taxable event is the payment of wages. Taxes can be direct and indirect.

Direct taxation is defined by being personalized and progressive, and by being levied according to the taxpayer's income or property value. Income Tax (IR) and Urban Property Tax (IPTU) are examples of direct taxes.

Indirect taxes are defined by being impersonal and regressive and by being levied equally on all taxpayers regardless of the taxpayer's income or property value. Airport Boarding Fees (TE), State Goods and Services Tax (ICMS) and Social Security Contribution (INSS) are examples of indirect taxes.

Regressive tax rates charged to taxpayers are the same for the rich, the poor and the middle class. For example, if someone spends R$400.00 per month on fuel for their car, 18% ICMS is R$87.80 per month (400.00/0.82 = 487.80 – 400.00 = 87.80), and that amount is exactly the same for all individuals, whether they are poor, middle class or rich. This monthly ICMS amount of R$87.80 per month is equivalent to 6.271428% of the income of a person earning R$1,400.00 per month and 0.627142% of the income of a person earning R$14,000.00 per month. Therefore, it is regressive because it is more costly for those who earn less and less costly for those who earn more.

Brazil's current tax system (as of February 2023), with its 92 levies, is very complicated and confusing. That is why legal entities (companies) needed to create tax accounting, also known as fiscal accounting, to oversee all of the procedures necessary for collecting the taxes embedded into the prices of products, goods and services sold.

ADMINISTRATIVE AND POLITICAL REFORM

DEFINITIONS:

Single-member district voting for each municipality: Each electoral district has the same number of voters and elects one legislative representative to the Municipal Council. The number of electoral districts in each municipality is the result of dividing the total number of voters in the municipality by the total number of councilmen in the municipality. Voters vote only for candidates from the electoral district to which they belong. The Municipal Council elects a council member to be the municipal mayor.

Single-member district voting for each state: Each electoral district has the same number of voters and elects one legislative representative to the State Legislature. The number of electoral districts in each state is the result of dividing the total number of voters in the state by the total number of seats in the State Legislature. Voters vote only for candidates from the electoral district to which they belong. The State Legislature elects a state legislator to be governor.

Single-member district voting for the House of Representatives: Each electoral district has the same number of voters and elects one legislative representative to the House of Representatives. The number of electoral districts is the result of dividing the total number of voters in the country by the total number of federal representatives in the House of Representatives. Voters vote only for candidates from the electoral district to which they belong.

Single-member district voting for the Senate: Each electoral district has the same number of voters and elects one representative to the Senate. The number of electoral districts is the result of dividing the total number of voters in the country by the total number of senators. Voters vote only for candidates from the district to which they belong.

Algorithm: Logical sequence of instructions for the electronic processing system to produce a certain result. For example, to calculate 2 x 3 = 6, the computer programmer writes a logical sequence of instructions in programming language, equivalent to what you do with a manual calculator when you press the keys (2), (x), (3) and (=), to get 6.

TRANSPARENCY

All federal government expenditures made with public funds will have to be fully transparent and available online, with a description and total amount of the expenditure for each item. The descriptions of each public expenditure must contain all information necessary to be examined and audited by any interested person. Additional information can be requested by anyone and must be delivered to the interested person within forty-eight hours of such request. Information regarding the administrative activities of the federal government cannot be kept secret, without exception.

Federal District: Under this tax reform, the federal district will be considered a state.

The definitions of the revenue sources (collection) for the federal, state and local governments are the amounts of the Single Tax (IU) that each of these governments is responsible for.

ADMINISTRATIVE AND POLITICAL REFORM

This reform will institute a republican parliamentarianism system with single-member district voting, five-year terms for elected officials and a ban on reelection. Republican parliamentarianism is an administrative and political representative democracy system defined by a government whose authority is derived from the consent of the people, in which citizens elect representatives to act on their political behalf. The parliamentary system is better than the presidential system for two reasons: (a) a president elected by parliament only acts as a formal representative of the country, and (b) the Executive Branch is headed by a Prime Minister, who is a parliamentarian elected by the parliamentarians themselves and granted executive powers to govern the country. Therefore, there are no power struggles with another branch of government, as is the case in the presidential system, which creates power struggles between the Legislative and Executive branches, especially in the drafting and execution of the annual budget. If lawmakers are not satisfied with the way the prime minister is running the country, they can remove the prime minister through a vote of no confidence, and elect another lawmaker for the position, swiftly and without any political trauma, as opposed to the lengthy and traumatic process of impeaching a president under the presidential system. Republican parliamentarianism will also be the political system of states and municipalities. Parliamentarians may not be penalized if they do not follow the guidelines and instructions of party leaders before each vote, to ensure that there is no interference in how they perform their role.

PURPOSE OF GOVERNMENT

The purpose of the federal, state and local governments is to collect taxes for the exclusive purpose of providing public services to the population; therefore, once this reform is approved and implemented, governments will be prohibited from engaging in business activities in the service, industrial and commercial sectors. Consequently, these same governments must privatize all of their state-owned enterprises, without exception, and must also sell all of their real estate, equipment, machinery and vehicles that are not necessary for the provision of public services to the populations in their jurisdictions within five years after this administrative reform is approved and implemented.

FEDERAL GOVERNMENT

The federal government shall consist of the office of the prime minister and the following ministries:

Ministry of Social Security

Planning and administration of the National Social Security Policy, through the National

Institute of Social Security (INSS). Planning and execution of the Universal Basic Income policy of one minimum monthly wage for each family, which will replace unemployment insurance, all pensions paid with public funds, and all other social welfare programs currently in place. The law will prohibit the government from creating a waiting line for applications for universal basic income of one minimum wage for each family.

Ministry of Health

Planning and execution of the National Public Health Policy, leadership and interstate coordination of the National Public Health Policy and provision of vaccines and continuous medication at no cost to states.

Ministry of the Environment

Planning and execution of the National Policy for the protection and preservation of the environment, and repression of criminal activities that destroy the environment.

Ministry of Economy

Planning and execution of National Economic Policy, administration of the National Revenue

Service and the Brazilian Institute of Geography and Statistics (IBGE).

Ministry of Justice

Planning and execution of the Federal Justice, which will receive and judge only federal crimes punishable by prison sentences, and administration of the Federal Police and the Brazilian Intelligence Agency (ABIN). All actions not punishable by prison sentences will be mediated and arbitrated by private courts through the municipal Mediation and Arbitration Chambers and the municipal Arbitration Court. Only cases that are not settled after two mediation hearings will be accepted for submission to arbitration. The highest level of Private Justice is the municipal Arbitration Court. The only federal offenses punishable by prison sentences are crimes against people and public and private property crimes. These crimes are imprescriptible and the sentence for them is financial reparation for the damage caused, and, when the criminal action results in death, financial reparation is paid to the family of the deceased. Only repeat offenders will be sentenced to prison.

Ministry of Defense

Planning and execution of the National Internal and External Defense Policy and provision of specific defense services as provided by law.

Ministry of Infrastructure

Planning and execution of the National Infrastructure Policy, leadership and interstate coordination of the National Infrastructure Policy.

Ministry of International Relations

Planning and execution of the National Policy on International Relations and planning and execution of the International and National Tourism Policy.

Ministry of Science, Technology and Innovation

Planning and execution of the National Policy for Science, Technology, Innovation and Vocational Education. Planning and administration of Research Institutes, Federal Universities and Technical Schools. In-person school attendance is optional, but tests must be taken in person. Tuition is free only for students from families who earn up to twice the minimum monthly wage.

CENTRAL BANK OF BRAZIL

The Central Bank of Brazil will be responsible for planning and executing the National Monetary Policy, printing paper money and minting coins, regulating and monitoring national banks, intervening in national banks in serious situations, supervising the Brazilian Payment System (SPB), for executing the National Monetary Policy, and for the National Exchange Policy. The administrative transparency rules of the Central Bank of Brazil are the same as the administrative transparency rules of the federal government.

FEDERAL SUPREME COURT

The Federal Supreme Court will only hear and decide cases involving questions about the Brazilian constitution. Federal criminal actions liable to prison sentences will be heard and decided by lower courts of the Federal Justice system, and actions not punishable by prison sentences will be heard, mediated, and arbitrated by the Private Justice system, through the municipal mediation and arbitration chambers created in the municipalities. The administrative transparency standards of the Supreme Court are the same as those of the federal government.

LEGISLATIVE POWER

Drafting and passing laws, modify existing laws, repeal existing laws, and governing the country through the prime minister. If the prime minister's performance is deemed inadequate, he/she can be removed from office at any time, swiftly and without any political trauma, by the lawmakers themselves, through a vote of no-confidence; in a new vote, another lawmaker will be elected as prime minister. In case of a political crisis where parliament fails to achieve the majority of votes necessary to elect a parliamentarian as the new prime minister, the President will dissolve parliament and call for general elections to elect new members. The new parliament will then choose another lawmaker as the new prime minister. The administrative transparency standards of the legislative branch are the same as the administrative transparency standards of the federal government.

PUBLIC SERVANTS

All public servants will be hired through public service exams and no one may become a public servant without first passing such exams or having been elected to public office, as provided by law, and, in the latter case, any assistants hired by such elected officials must be public servants who have passed public service exams. Therefore, all so-called positions of trust are prohibited, because all public servants who have passed public service exams are trustworthy.

All public servants will have thirty days of vacation time per year, without exceptions; such vacation time must be used annually.

Monthly salaries for all public servants, without exceptions, will be at least equivalent to twice the minimum monthly wage, and at most, equivalent to 10x the minimum monthly wage. Anyone who finds that such compensation is not enough can always choose not to take a public service exam to work for the government.

Public servants are prohibited from using government vehicles for personal transportation, except in cases provided by law for safety reasons. All public servants, without exception, are prohibited from using corporate credit and debit cards. Public servants, without exceptions, who travel on business will receive a travel per diem and, upon returning from the business trip, must submit receipts for their expenses attached to the travel expenses report and, as appropriate, receive or return the difference between the travel per diem they received before traveling and the expenses incurred during the business trip. A public servant who is transferred to work in another city will receive one month's rent allowance and this amount will be excluded from the maximum monthly salary. Public servants can only be dismissed following the conclusion of an administrative process that assures the public servant the right to defense and appeal.

Effectiveness of this administrative reform: Given the vested rights of public servants employed in their current positions, this administrative reform will only apply to future public servants who are hired to new positions after this administrative reform is approved.

Vested rigth: Legal right that comes from a legal fact that has been legally consummated and that can no longer be taken away from the individual, even if a new law provides otherwise, because the right was acquired before a new law took effect.

E-GOVERNMENT

Implementation of e-government, using artificial intelligence algorithms to automate all the administrative work of the federal government that is still being done manually by public servants. The job of public servants will be to input data, when necessary, so that the electronic processing system outputs and provides all the results programmed in the artificial intelligence algorithms of the electronic processing system, to be used by public servants to offer public services to the population.

Federal government revenue source: Total amount of Single Tax (IU) payable to the federal government.

STATE GOVERNMENTS

State governments will consist of the governor's office and the following departments:

Department of Health

Planning and execution of the state's public health policy, delivery of vaccines and continuous medication at no cost to municipalities, and inter-municipal coordination of the municipal public health programs.

Department of the Economy

Planning and execution of state tax collection, planning and coordination of the state's economic policy, and inter-municipal coordination of the state's economic policy.

Department of Infrastructure

Planning and execution of the state's public infrastructure policy, and inter-municipal coordination of municipal infrastructure policies.

Department of Science, Technology and Innovation

Planning and execution of the state policy for science, technology, innovation and vocational education. Planning and administration of research institutes, State Universities and Technical Schools. In-person school attendance is optional, but tests must be taken in person. Tuition is free only for students from families who earn up to twice the minimum monthly wage.

Department of Justice

Planning and execution of the State Justice, which will only decide on state crimes punishable by prison sentences. All other actions will be heard by the Private Justice system, through the municipal Mediation and Arbitration Chambers and the Municipal Arbitration Court. Only cases that are not settled after two mediation hearings will be accepted for submission to arbitration. The highest level of Private Justice is the municipal Arbitration Court. The state courts will continue to rely on the State Civil Police as the judicial police. The state military police will cease to exist, and its current officers will be transferred to the municipalities, under the municipal civil police departments. Current state military police officers will be transferred to the municipalities in proportion to the number of inhabitants in each municipality. The former military police officers and the current officers of the municipal civil police departments will receive specific training in each municipality to serve as municipal civil police officers. The only state crimes punishable by prison sentences are crimes against people and public and private property crimes. These crimes are imprescriptible and the sentence for them is financial reparation for the damage caused, and, when the criminal action results in death, financial reparation is paid to the family of the deceased. Only repeat offenders will be sentenced to prison.

E-GOVERNMENT

Implementation of e-government, using artificial intelligence algorithms to automate all the administrative work of the state government that is still being done manually by public servants. The job of public servants will be to input data, when necessary, so that the electronic processing system outputs and provides all the results programmed in the artificial intelligence algorithms of the electronic processing system, to be used by public servants to offer public services to the population.

TRANSPARENCY

All government expenditures made by the state with public funds will have to be fully transparent and available online, with a description and total amount of the expenditure for each item. The descriptions of each public expenditure must contain all information necessary to be examined and audited by any interested person. Additional information can be requested by anyone and must be delivered to the interested person within forty-eight hours of such request. Information regarding the administrative activities of state governments cannot be kept secret, without exception.

State government revenue source: Total amount of Single Tax (IU) payable to each state government.

Municipal governments will consist of the mayor's office and the following departments:

Department of Health

Planning and execution of the municipal health policy, and administration of the municipal public health clinics and municipal public hospitals. Municipalities that do not have a municipal hospital will enter into an agreement to use the nearest municipal hospital.

Department of Teaching

Planning and execution of the municipal public policy for free elementary school education. In-person attendance is optional, but tests must be taken in person. The current Education Department will cease to exist, because parents are responsible for educating their children.

Department of the Economy

Planning and execution of municipal economic policy, and administration of municipal revenue.

Department of Labor

Planning and execution of the municipal policy to promote employment and work.

Department of Science, Technology and Innovation

Planning and execution of the municipal policy for science, technology, innovation, and vocational education, and drafting of municipal master plan for each elective period, with approval for each government project, to ensure that only projects that are part of the municipal master plan are executed, to avoid the appropriation of government spending for projects that serve special interests within a district.

Department of Infrastructure

Planning and execution of the municipal public infrastructure policy.

Department of Public Safety

Planning and execution of municipal public security policy, through the municipal Civil Police, and administration of the prison. Repeat offenders of crimes against people and public and private property who are sentenced to prison by the federal and state courts will serve their prison sentences in the municipal prison. While serving their sentences, these repeat offenders are required to undergo a six-month treatment administered by charismatic religious preachers, in order to convert them into law-abiding citizens. If this treatment does not achieve the expected result, repeat offenders will undergo a six-month hypnotic therapy treatment administered by psychiatrists. If this treatment also fails to convert repeat offenders into law-abiding citizens they will be locked up, not in prison cells, but in the common areas of prisons until the progress of human knowledge finds the means to convert them into law-abiding people or until they die. In these walled prisons, prisoners will live on their own and will receive only medical and dental care, and no other assistance, and will have to plant, grow, harvest and prepare their own food, and do all other work necessary for their survival.

Municipalities that do not have prisons will enter into an agreement to use the nearest municipal prison.

Private Justice Department

Authorization and supervision of the Mediation and Arbitration Chambers and the municipal Arbitration Court, which will receive all cases not punishable by prison sentences, for mediation and arbitration. Authorization and supervision of the Mediation and Arbitration Chambers and the municipal Arbitration Court, which will receive all cases not punishable by prison sentences, for mediation and arbitration. The appointment of attorneys of the parties to serve in the Mediation and Arbitration Chambers and in the Arbitration Court is optional. Cases punishable by prison sentences must be heard in federal or state courts.

E-GOVERNMENT

Implementation of e-government, using artificial intelligence algorithms to automate all the administrative work of municipal governments that is still being done manually by public servants. The job of public servants will be to input data, when necessary, so that the electronic processing system outputs and provides all the results programmed in the artificial intelligence algorithms of the electronic processing system, to be used by public servants to offer public services to the population.

TRANSPARENCY

All municipal government expenditures made with public funds will have to be fully transparent and available online, with a description and total amount of the expenditure for each item. The descriptions of each public expenditure must contain all information necessary to be examined and audited by any interested person. Additional information can be requested by anyone and must be delivered to the interested person within forty-eight hours of such request. Information regarding the administrative activities of municipal governments cannot be kept secret, without exception.

Municipal government revenue source: Total amount of Single Tax (IU) payable to each municipal government.

ELECTORAL SYSTEM

Single-member district voting, under republican parliamentarism.

The right to vote, as opposed to the duty to vote.

Five-year term and ban on reelection for all elected offices.

Acceptance of independent candidates without any affiliation to political parties. Acceptance of independent candidates affiliated to political parties who were not selected in party primaries to run for state representative, senator, state legislators and city council members.

Ban on public funding and ban on corporate funding for political parties and electoral campaigns.

Individuals may donate up to a maximum of 10x the minimum monthly wage per individual (per CPF) to political parties and electoral campaigns.

Direct elections, through electronic polling machines, immediately following municipal elections, or through the internet, for the following offices:

Justice of the Federal Supreme Court.
Justice of the Superior Court of Justice.
Judges of Federal, District and State Appellate Courts.
Federal, District, State and Municipal Attorneys General.

Federal Police Commissioner.
Director of the Brazilian Intelligence Agency
State and Municipal Civil Police Commissioner.
President of Regulatory Agencies.
President of the Central Bank.

For the elections for the Justices of the Federal Supreme Court and the Superior Court of Justice, as well as for Regional Court judges, the electorate consists of all judges residing in their jurisdictions. Each of these voters has the right to be a candidate in this election. For the Attorneys General elections, the electorate consists of all prosecutors working in their jurisdictions, and each of the voters has the right to be a candidate in this election. For the election for the Federal Police commissioner and the director of the Brazilian Intelligence Agency, the electorate consists of all federal police officers, and each of these voters has the right to be a candidate in this election. For the election for the State and Municipal Civil Police commissioners, the electorate consists of all civil police officers in the Civil Police departments of the jurisdictions, and each of these voters has the right to be a candidate in this election.

For the election for president of each Regulatory Agency, the electorate consists of all professionals in the field of each Regulatory Agency, and each of these voters has the right to be a candidate in this election. For the election for president of the Central Bank, the electorate consists of the Ministry of Treasury of the federal government, the state treasury secretaries, and each of these voters has the right to be a candidate in this election.

CURRENT ADMINISTRATIVE AND POLITICAL SYSTEM

FEDERAL GOVERNMENT

The current federal political system is a presidential system, which allows the president to be reelected once. In this political system, the Executive Power is exercised by the president as granted by the Federal Constitution, in accordance with the laws and the annual budget approved by the Legislative Branch.

Since real power, de facto power, lies with the Legislative Branch, the presidential system of government leads to power struggles between the

Executive and the Legislative Branches, especially when it comes to drafting and executing the annual budget, and such disputes undermine the country's governability.

Real power lies with the legislative because it is the branch that drafts and approves amendments to the Federal Constitution, except for the unamendable articles. It also drafts and approves new laws, and modifies and repeals existing laws. These are the laws that govern the behavior of all people in their social and institutional interrelationships. In other words, the laws that shape all social interaction determine how the president governs the country, how judges rule, and even how legislators legislate.

STATE GOVERNMENTS

The current political system in the states is similar to the presidential system of the federal government, allowing governors to be reelected once. In this political system, executive power is exercised by the governors as granted by the state constitutions, in accordance with the laws and annual budget approved by state legislative branches.

Since real power lies with the Legislative Branch, the current system of government in the states leads to power struggles between the Executive and the Legislative Branches, especially when it comes to drawing up and executing the annual budget, and such disputes undermine governability for the states.

Real power lies with the legislative because it is the branch that drafts and approves amendments to state constitutions, drafts and approves new laws, and modifies and repeals existing laws. These are the laws that govern the behavior of all people in their social and institutional interrelationships. In other words, the laws that shape all social interaction determine how governors govern the states, how judges rule, and even how legislators legislate.

MUNICIPAL GOVERNMENTS

The current political system of the municipalities is similar to the presidential system of the federal government, which allows mayors to be reelected once. In this political system, the executive power is exercised by the mayors, who govern in accordance with the laws and annual budgets approved by their legislative branches.

Since real power lies with the Legislative Branch, the current system of government in the municipalities leads to power struggles between the Executive and the Legislative Branches, especially when it comes to drawing up and executing the annual budget, and such disputes undermine governability for the municipalities.

Real power lies with the legislative because it is the branch that drafts and approves amendments to municipal law, drafts and approves new laws, and modifies and repeals existing laws. Municipal laws and other laws govern the behavior of all people in their social and institutional interrelationships. In other words, these laws shape all social interaction, determine how mayors govern, how mediators conduct mediations and how arbitrators conduct arbitrations in the chambers of mediation and arbitration of private municipal justice, and even how municipal legislators themselves legislate.

CURRENT ELECTORAL SYSTEM

Voters have the duty to vote and, if they fail to provide justification when they do not vote, they are punished with fines and administrative penalties, such as not being able to submit a bid in a public tender and not being able to get a passport and identity card.

Elections are indirect, because political parties choose the individuals who run for public office, and voters are only allowed to vote for one of these candidates.

Individuals affiliated with political parties who have not been selected as candidates by the parties are not permitted to run for office, and neither are independent individuals who are not affiliated with any political parties.

Taxpayers bear a heavy burden for the current electoral system, as billions of reais of public money are spent to fund political parties and electoral campaigns.

Elected officials are allowed to be reelected once. Reelection is harmful to the population because the president, governors and mayors govern while thinking about their reelections and, consequently, fail to do what needs to be done for the good of the population in the medium and long term.

<table>
<tr><td>Title</td><td>REFORMS: TAX,
ADMINISTRATIVE AND
POLITICAL</td></tr>
<tr><td>Format</td><td>10,5 x 14,8cm</td></tr>
<tr><td>Typography texts</td><td>Minion Pro</td></tr>
<tr><td>Typography titles</td><td>**Roboto Slab**</td></tr>
<tr><td>Layout</td><td>Israel Dias de Oliveira</td></tr>
<tr><td>Translation</td><td>Icaro Bagolan</td></tr>
<tr><td>Revision</td><td>Débora Beltrão</td></tr>
</table>